Wild Britain

Rabbit

9

Louise and Richard Spilsbury

D0332755

H www.heinemann.co.uk
Visit our website to find out more information about Heinemann Library books.

To order:
☎ Phone 44 (0) 1865 888066
📄 Send a fax to 44 (0) 1865 314091
💻 Visit the Heinemann Bookshop at www.heinemann.co.uk to browse our catalogue and order online.

First published in Great Britain by Heinemann Library, Halley Court, Jordan Hill, Oxford OX2 8EJ, part of Harcourt Education Ltd. Heinemann is a registered trademark of Harcourt Education Ltd.

Editorial: Lucy Thunder and Helen Cannons
Design: David Poole and Celia Floyd
Illustrations: Jeff Edwards, Alan Fraser and Geoff Ward
Picture Research: Rebecca Sodergren and Peter Morris
Production: Edward Moore

Originated by Repro Multi-Warna
Printed and bound in China by South China Printing Company

The paper used to print this book comes from sustainable resources.

ISBN 0 431 03980 1 (hardback)
08 07 06 05 04
10 9 8 7 6 5 4 3 2 1

ISBN 0 431 03987 9 (paperback)
09 08 07 06 05
10 9 8 7 6 5 4 3 2 1

British Library Cataloguing in Publication Data
Spilsbury, Louise and Spilsbury, Richard
Rabbit. – (Wild britain)
599.3'22'0941

A full catalogue record for this book is available from the British Library.

Acknowledgements

The Publishers would like to thank the following for permission to reproduce photographs:

Ardea/D. Avon p28; Ardea/Bob Gibbons p26; Ardea/Stefan Meyers p6; Bruce Coleman/Jane Burton pp11, 25; Bruce Coleman/William S. Paton p21; Bruce Coleman/Colin Varndell p22; DK Images p20; FLPA/Michael Clark p29; FLPA / H. Keher/J.B./Foto Natura p5; FLPA/Derek Middleton p13; NHPA/Manfred Danegger p12; NHPA/Mike Lane p15; NHPA/Michael Leach p19; NHPA/Allan Williams p10; Oxford Scientific Films pp16, 17, 18, 19, 23, 24; Pictor International p27; Windrush Photos/D. Mason p14; Woodfall Wild Images p8; Woodfall Wild Images/Mark Hamblin p4; Woodfall Wild Images/John Robinson p9.

Cover photograph of a rabbit resting in its natural habitat, reproduced with permission of Woodfall Wild Images/Mike Lane.

The Publishers would like to thank Michael Scott for his assistance in the preparation of this book.

Every effort has been made to contact copyright holders of any material reproduced in this book. Any omissions will be rectified in subsequent printings if notice is given to the Publisher.

Contents

Any words appearing in the text in bold, **like this**, are explained in the Glossary.

What are rabbits?

Most wild rabbits have sandy brown, grey or dark brown hair on their body.

Rabbits are a kind of **mammal**. Wild rabbits are similar to rabbits that people keep as pets. They have long ears, long back legs and a fluffy tail.

Adult rabbits like these grow to about 40 centimetres long. Can you tell that the male is on the right?

Male rabbits are usually slightly bigger and heavier than female rabbits. **Female** rabbits have a narrower head.

Where do rabbits live?

Rabbits live in all sorts of quiet, grassy places.

Rabbits live in hedgerows, fields and woodlands. They also live in **sand dunes**, by railway lines, canals, parks, gardens and churchyards.

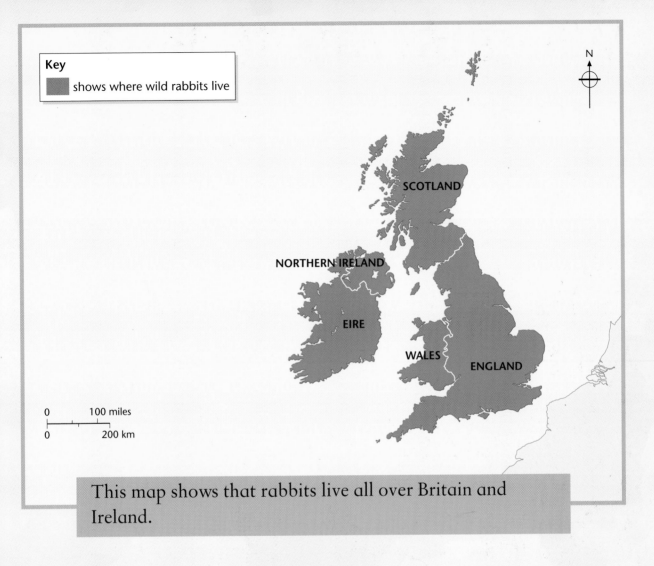

Key

shows where wild rabbits live

SCOTLAND

NORTHERN IRELAND

EIRE

WALES

ENGLAND

0   100 miles

0   200 km

This map shows that rabbits live all over Britain and Ireland.

Rabbits first came to Britain about 800 years ago. People brought them from France and kept them for their fur and meat. By 200 years ago, wild rabbits had spread all over Britain.

What do rabbits eat?

When lots of rabbits feed in the same place, they help to keep the grass short.

Rabbits eat only plants. They eat many different kinds of plants, including grass. Rabbits eat plant leaves and other parts, such as **roots** and **shoots**.

A rabbit's sharp front teeth are good for biting. The teeth inside the mouth are good for chewing.

Plants are tough to eat, so rabbits have strong teeth to eat them with. They use their teeth to chew grass and bite through hard roots.

Finding food

Rabbits have large eyes that help them see in dim light.

Rabbits usually feed at dusk or dawn. It is safer then because **predators** cannot see them so easily. In places where rabbits feel safer, they feed in the daytime as well.

Rabbits use their long ears to listen out for danger before they leave their burrows.

Rabbits look for food near a hedgerow, their **burrow** or other safe places. This means they can run to safety if a predator appears.

11

On the move

Rabbits hop away very quickly when they are in danger.

Rabbits can hop slowly or leap along very quickly. They have strong back legs to help them hop. The big feet on their back legs give them an extra push as they leap.

When rabbits go underneath fences, their hair sometimes catches on the wire.

Rabbits move along the same paths to feeding areas. They often travel along fences or hedgerows. These help them to hide from **predators**.

Rabbit groups

These rabbits come from the same warren. There may be hundreds of rabbits in one warren.

Wild rabbits live together in groups. They live in **warrens**. A warren is a set of underground **burrows**. Tunnels connect the burrows to each other.

Warrens have many entrance holes so that if a **predator** goes into one, the rabbits can escape through another!

Rabbit warrens can be very large and deep. Most warrens have lots of different burrows. They also have many different entrance holes so rabbits can come and go quickly.

Inside a rabbit warren

A rabbit's whiskers help it to feel its way in the dark tunnels of a warren.

Female rabbits dig most of the tunnels in a **warren**. The tunnels are about 15 centimetres wide – just big enough for a rabbit to squeeze through!

This rabbit is washing itself in the safety of its burrow.

In their **burrows**, rabbits dig out rooms to rest and sleep in. Underground burrows keep rabbits warm and dry. They also keep rabbits safely hidden from **predators**.

17

Rabbit young

This mother rabbit is collecting dry grass for her nest. This will keep the babies warm and comfy.

Female rabbits dig out special holes to have their babies in. They make a nest in a hole inside their **burrow**. They use grass, moss and hair from their belly to make the nest.

Baby rabbits are called kittens. They are helpless and their mother must take care of them.

A mother rabbit usually has five or six babies at a time. When baby rabbits are born their eyes are closed, they cannot hear and they have no hair to keep them warm.

Growing up

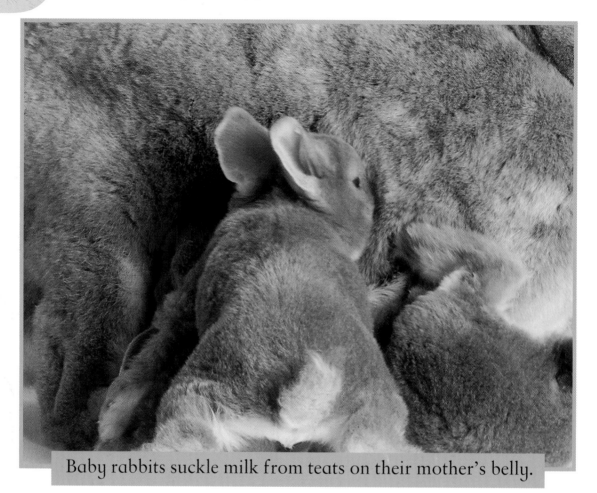

Baby rabbits suckle milk from teats on their mother's belly.

At first the baby rabbits feed on their mother's milk. This is called **suckling**. The mother leaves the babies in the nest. She visits once or twice a day to feed them.

Young rabbits will be grown up when they are about four months old. Then they can have babies of their own.

Baby rabbits have hair by eight days old. By ten days old their eyes are open. At about three weeks old they leave the **burrow** and start to eat plants.

21

Rabbit sounds and smells

When a rabbit thumps its back legs on the ground, other rabbits can easily hear the sound.

Rabbits make sounds that other rabbits can hear. They thump their back legs on the ground. This makes a loud noise that tells other rabbits that danger is near.

This rabbit is rubbing its chin on a low branch to leave its smell. Rabbits feel safe in places they have marked like this.

Rabbits recognize each other by their smell. They also use smell to mark where they live. They leave droppings and rub their chin against things to leave their smell on them.

Under attack

Buzzards in the sky look out for animals, like young rabbits, below. Then they swoop down and catch them.

Badgers, buzzards and weasels try to catch and eat young rabbits. Foxes, cats, stoats and polecats eat adult rabbits, too. Few wild rabbits live for more than two years.

When rabbits run off, their white tail tells other rabbits to run, too.

When rabbits run away from a **predator** the white fluffy part of their tail shows. This tells other rabbits that danger is near and it is time to run.

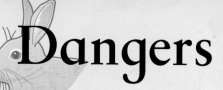

Dangers

This is a trap to catch rabbits that have been eating a gardener's plants.

In places where many rabbits live near people, they can become pests. They eat plants that farmers and gardeners grow. Some people trap or shoot rabbits.

If you see a wild rabbit by a road or path, do not touch it. Once you have gone, it will run back to its **burrow**.

Wild rabbits look like pet rabbits, but you should not touch them. Some wild rabbits have a **disease** that makes them very sick. It could make you ill, too.

A rabbit's year

In spring it is easy for young rabbits, like these, to find food.

Most baby rabbits are born in spring and summer. This is when plants have most leaves and flowers. Young rabbits need to eat a lot when they first leave the **burrow**.

A rabbit's strong teeth help it to bite bark off trees. This apple tree was damaged by rabbits.

In winter there is less food for rabbits. Leaves fall from plants and snow may cover the grass. In winter rabbits often eat **bark** from young trees.

Animal groups

Scientists group together animals that are similar. Rabbits are in the same group as hares. Both eat only plants and have a second set of smaller front teeth behind the main pair.

hare

rabbit

The artwork on this page is not to scale.

Glossary

bark   tough outer layer around the main part of a tree

burrows   underground holes that rabbits dig out to live in

disease   something that stops an animal's body from working properly and makes them ill

female   animal that can become a mother when it is grown up

male   animal that can become a father when it is grown up

mammals   group of animals that includes humans. All mammals feed their babies their own milk and have some hair on their bodies.

predators   animals that catch other animals to eat them

roots   parts of a plant that grow below the ground. Roots take in water and goodness from the soil to help a plant grow.

sand dunes   small hills of sand that pile up behind a beach

scientist   person who studies the world around us and the things in it to find out how they work

shoot   young stem of a plant

suckling   when a mammal mother feeds her baby with milk from her body. A baby rabbit sucks milk from teats on its mother's tummy.

warrens   grouping of underground rabbit burrows linked by tunnels

Index